C000314813

A cuppa
and a prayer

reflections on daily life

**kevin
mayhew**

First published in 2006 by

KEVIN MAYHEW LTD
Buxhall, Stowmarket, Suffolk, IP14 3BW
E-mail: info@kevinmayhewltd.com
Website: www.kevinmayhew.com

9 8 7 6 5 4 3 2 1 0

ISBN 1 84417 520 0
Catalogue No. 1500879

Designed by Chris Coe

Printed and bound in China

Contents

Introduction

Where do we find inspiration for prayer and when do we find time actually to pray? Many of us look for a quiet slot when, for a few moments, we can focus on God's presence, whether that is first thing in the morning, during the evening after the children have gone to bed, or last thing at night before we go to sleep. Such moments are important if our spiritual life is to stay strong, for without them God can all too easily be crowded out, but that shouldn't mean prayer has no place in the rest of life. He is as much present in run-of-the-mill experiences as anywhere, if only we have eyes to see him, and sometimes it is ordinary moments that can speak most powerfully to us, suggesting areas for reflection.

This book offers a selection of prayers taken from three of my recent publications, each drawing inspiration from everyday experiences in and around the home, from the routine drudgery of housework and shopping, to relaxing in front of the TV, to sitting down with a newspaper or good book and a nice hot cuppa. Instead of seeing prayer as a retreat into some private spiritual world, it emphasises God's involvement in every aspect of life, however mundane it may seem. It is my hope that something in these pages will prove of help to you in deepening your relationship with God in the press of a busy day.

Nick Fawcett

The cup of tea

I poured it out eagerly,
  dying for a cuppa to quench my thirst ...
  but then spat it out,
  grimacing in disgust.
It was tepid,
  neither hot nor cold,
  fit only for the kitchen sink,
  to where it was swiftly dispatched.

Lord, my faith blows hot and cold,
  sometimes setting me on fire with enthusiasm,
  at others, ardour cooled almost to zero,
  but more often —
  too often —
  I'm like that cup of tea:
  lukewarm,
  little use to you or anyone.
Kindle afresh a fire of devotion in my heart,
  and fan there a burning desire
  to love and serve you better.

Amen.

The armchair

It was comfortable —
  too comfortable —
  enticing me simply to lie back,
  relax
  and let the world go by.
Nothing wrong with that, of course,
  for work without rest is no good to anyone,
  but I also need exercise and activity,
  those equally vital if I hope to stay in shape.

Forgive, Lord, my laziness in discipleship,
  my inclination to lounge in the comfort zone
  rather than stretch the muscles of faith.
Forgive me for reducing what ought to be a way of life
  to a casual pursuit,
  a couch potato commitment that asks little
  and delivers less.
Teach me to work at my faith,
  so that it not only shapes every aspect of life
  but is also kept in shape in turn.

Amen.

The housework

They spoke to me, that day —
   the washing on the line,
   the pile of dishes,
   the neatly ironed clothes
   and the smell of cooking —
   jobs done out of necessity
   but also out of love —
   and as that truth sank home
I thought of the countless deeds I take for granted,
   small in themselves
   but contributing so much to my comfort and happiness,
   and signifying devotion in a way beyond words.

Forgive me, Lord, for failing to appreciate my loved ones,
   slow not simply to show my gratitude
   but even to notice the innumerable ways they enrich my life.
Teach me to recognise everything they do
   and, in word and deed, to show how much it means.

Amen.

The letter

Hadn't I replied?
I'd meant to,
   lots of times,
   but never got round to it,
   the letter sitting there in silent accusation,
   as though reproaching me for my failure to answer.
I had my reasons, of course —
   distractions, demands, you know the sort of thing —
   but they didn't wash,
   for I'd promised to reply
   and I hadn't.

Forgive me, Lord, for I mean to answer you —
   to acknowledge your goodness,
   pass on my thanks,
   respond to your call —
   but so often I'm found wanting.
And whatever excuses I make,
   they don't hold water,
   for no concern, however pressing,
   should be more important than you.
Teach me to make time for you
   as you have made time for me.

Amen.

The postcard

It didn't show much —
   just a stretch of hills,
   section of cliffs
   and expanse of sea —
   yet it gave an idea of where we were staying,
   enough to give a feel of the place,
   a glimpse of its peace and sense of its beauty.

Lord, you have given a glimpse of your kingdom
   through the life of Christ and the witness of Scripture.
Not a complete portrait,
   still less every detail,
   but enough to give an impression of its splendour,
   a flavour of the joy, refreshment and tranquillity
   it holds in store.
May that glimpse capture my imagination
   and sustain my faith,
   this and every day.

Amen.

The noisy neighbour

He swayed in time with the music,
    exulting in the pounding rhythm,
    the remorseless throb of the drums,
    lost in the music's power,
    but next door the exhausted baby screamed in protest,
    the mother nursed her headache, blinking back tears,
    and the father hammered despairingly on the partition wall —
    so thin a divide between heaven and hell.

In so many things, Lord,
    more than I realise,
    my pleasure comes at the expense of others,
    what brings **me** joy causing **them** pain.
Teach me, in all I do,
    however innocent it may seem,
    to consider its impact on those around me,
    and, where necessary, to put their wishes before my own.

Amen.

The window cleaner

I was ashamed when he'd finished,
   appalled that so much dirt could have built up without me
   noticing,
   clouding my vision and obscuring the view.
Suddenly the sun seemed brighter,
   colours enriched,
   little details previously hidden now noticed,
   everything fresh,
   made new.

Wipe clear, Lord, the windows of my soul,
   so that, seeing you better,
   I may know you more fully.
Grant me a clearer picture of you
   that sheds new light on every aspect of life,
   every part transformed by your sanctifying touch.

Amen.

The charity appeal

It was another appeal,
   yet one more begging letter thrust through my door,
   tugging at the heartstrings and seeking my support.
A worthy cause, no doubt,
   as deserving as any other,
   but I'd done my bit, hadn't I? –
   already given more than generously.
What more could people ask?

Is that true, Lord?
Have I done enough?
I've given, certainly,
   but was each donation a meaningful gift
   or a token gesture,
   a response from the heart
   or an attempt to salve my conscience?
I've offered a little but no more,
   what I spare for others over a lifetime
   barely what I spend on myself in a week.
Forgive me,
   and teach me to deal generously,
   as you have dealt generously with me.

Amen.

The kitchen scales

Six ounces of sugar,
    six of flour,
    six more of margarine —
    carefully I weighed out the ingredients,
    resolved to get them right.
Too little of one,
    too much of another,
    and the balance would be skewed,
    the cake spoiled,
    my efforts a waste of time.

Teach me, Lord, to weigh up my life,
    assessing what goes into it
    and what comes out;
    to make time for work and rest,
    reflection and action,
    myself and others,
    this world and your kingdom.
Teach me to find a place for all,
    keeping each in balance with the rest,
    so that, from the ingredients you've given,
    I may make something special for you.

Amen.

The supermarket

Food, drink, clothes, books;
   houseware, electrical goods, even insurance –
   all there under one roof at bargain prices,
   everything we need,
   all we could ask for.
And crowds flocked accordingly to this consumer paradise,
   a cathedral of delights.

I'm not knocking it, Lord,
   for the bargains are welcome,
   the range excellent,
   and the convenience a bonus,
   but I can stack my trolley full
   yet still leave empty
   if I imagine what I buy can meet my needs.
It may feed the body
   but not the soul,
   delight the senses
   but not the spirit –
   contentment being a gift rather than product,
   a treasure to be received
   rather than commodity plucked from a shelf.
Teach me where true fulfilment lies,
   and to seek it before all else.

Amen.

The newspaper

I glimpsed the headline emblazoned over the front page —
   sensational stuff! —
   but shrugged indifferently and turned aside,
   for it was old hat,
   yesterday's paper,
   news no longer.
What excited once, bores now,
   what was fresh then, is stale now.

I glimpsed the message running through the pages,
   the Word made flesh,
   Christ crucified and risen —
   sensational stuff! —
   but once more I shrugged and turned aside,
   for again it was old hat,
   news no longer.
Only I was wrong,
   for it's as much today's news as yesterday's,
   as alive now as it will ever be,
   news for you, me and everyone.
Lord, keep me ever-enthused and excited by what you have done
   and continue to do through Christ my Lord.

Amen.

The bookmark

It marked my place in the book,
  showing how much I'd read
  and how much was left,
  saving me from the chore, after putting it aside,
  of thumbing through the pages to find the point I'd reached.

Though there's no such simple tool, Lord,
  in the unfolding story of faith,
  help me to gauge my progress there,
  recognising how far I've come
  and how far I've yet to go.
Save me from going back over the same old ground,
  settling for the familiar and undemanding,
  but save me also from getting ahead of myself,
  believing that the tale is complete when it's barely started.
Show me where I am,
  and where you would have me be,
  and, as I continue the saga of discipleship,
  help me to advance from one page to the other.

Amen.

The meal

They ate dutifully enough,
    smiling politely and making the odd appreciative noise,
    but I knew they were enjoying it no more than I was.
The meal was bland,
    all but tasteless,
    and with good reason,
    for I'd forgotten to add seasoning —
    so small an ingredient,
    so large an effect.

Forgive me, Lord, for the insipid fare I offer you,
    looking the part
    and with so many of the components right,
    yet lacking the one thing needful:
    the savour of love.
Teach me that the poorest of dishes
    with that one vital ingredient
    is worth far more than the finest of feasts without it.

Amen.

The text message

He texted me —
  nothing eloquent or fancy,
  just a simple message to stay in touch,
  a quick word to keep me in the picture,
  reinforcing the friendship we'd built up over the years.

Lord, teach me that staying in touch with you
  doesn't require special language
  or a formal approach,
  but is about a living relationship,
  making time to share every aspect of life,
  from the momentous to the mundane —
  the agony and ecstasy,
  triumphs and tribulations —
  each shared simply but sincerely
  in the knowledge that **they** matter to you because **I** matter.

Amen.

The cross-stitch

They were just a jumble of threads —
   no pattern to them,
   no order,
   no anything —
   but, having sketched out her design,
   she painstakingly wove them together,
   creating a thing of beauty,
   a unique and unforgettable work of art.

Thank you, Lord, for **your** creation:
   the beauty of this world and wonder of the universe.
Thank you for so much that speaks of your purpose,
   causing me to catch my breath in awe and wonder.
For the work of your hands
   and all it reveals of your love,
   receive my praise.

Amen.

The dust

It lay everywhere —
  thick upon each surface,
  each nook and cranny of the house —
  a sombre reminder of the fate we share:
  our striving and dreams,
  our very self,
  destined to turn to dust.

Yet from the dust of the earth, Lord,
  you fashioned our bodies and gave us life.
And though to the ground we return —
  dust to dust,
  ashes to ashes —
  you promise us new beginnings:
  love that will neither fade nor perish,
  a kingdom that never ends.
Speak then, not of death and decay,
  but of your new creation,
  life for evermore.

Amen.

The afternoon snooze

I tried to stay awake,
   fighting to control the creeping lethargy,
   but it was no good,
   the heavy meal and glass of wine,
   coupled with the summer heat,
   causing my head to nod and eyelids to droop,
   sleep closing in.

You, Lord, never tire or slumber.
Your love is constant each day,
   your faithfulness ever sure.
Whatever I face,
   you are there watching over me —
   guiding,
   protecting,
   loving,
   forgiving —
   your goodness never exhausted,
   your compassion never failing.
For that assurance, receive my praise.

Amen.

The headache tablet

It was nothing major,
   more of a dull ache than a pain,
   but I felt sorry for myself, nonetheless,
   enough to reach for the headache tablets
   and mope around miserably until the last trace had gone.

Forgive me, Lord,
   for I forget those who live in constant pain,
   longing for release yet finding no end to their suffering,
   each day blighted by its stranglehold.
Give them strength not just to get through
   but also to find joy and fulfilment in life,
   and grant the assurance that,
   just as you shared our sufferings in Christ,
   so, through him, we will all finally enter a brighter kingdom,
   in which pain and sorrow will be at an end.

Amen.

The feather duster

I rarely used it,
    but I should have done,
    for when I stopped to look there were cobwebs everywhere,
    trailing from the walls and ceiling in room after room,
    each a sign of complacency,
    of a spring-clean long overdue.

My faith, Lord, is cloaked with cobwebs,
    having been left untouched too often and for too long,
    neglected to the point of being redundant.
I've been complacent,
    assuming discipleship can look after itself,
    instead of needing a regular dusting down.
Forgive me,
    and may your Spirit sweep through my life,
    freshening up my faith
    and breathing new life within.

Amen.

The television

There are so many channels, Lord —
  movies, sport, history, news, and a host of others,
  each clamouring for my attention.
I could watch all of them so easily,
  but I don't want to,
  for they're finally about others,
  not me,
  proxy experiences, goals and achievements,
  surrogate thoughts and feelings.
I'll watch **some** programmes, of course,
  and enjoy them too —
  nothing wrong with that —
  but save me, Lord, from a second-hand existence,
  from spending too much time watching other people's lives
  and not enough living my own.

Amen.

The advertisements

It was laughable, really,
  the claims more exaggerated by the day:
  new,
  enhanced,
  improved;
  the most advanced formula ever,
  the finest and fastest of its kind;
  great value,
  great quality,
  great everything —
  quite simply, the best that money can buy.

Lord, I make extravagant claims —
  about the way you've changed my life,
  the person you've helped me become,
  and the life you've called me to lead.
Forgive me when the walk denies the talk,
  what people see in me
  leading them to dismiss the faith I profess
  as empty hype,
  more spin than substance.
Work within me,
  so that who I am may more closely resemble who
  you want me to be.

Amen.

The remote control

I flicked through channels,
   scrolled through text,
   recorded programmes,
   switched on and off,
   everything controlled at the touch of a button –
   volume, brightness, colour, contrast adjusted with ease
   without even moving from my chair.

Can't you, Lord, control this world you've made,
   putting an end to its hatred, sorrow, pain and death?
Can't you turn war to peace,
   evil to good,
   sickness to health
   and darkness to light,
   all at the touch of your hand?
But that's the wrong question, isn't it,
   for you **can** and **do** change things,
   only not remotely but by consent,
   not **controlling** what we do
   but **inviting** our response.
And though the price can be high
   I wouldn't have it any other way,
   for I'd much rather be a person than a puppet.
Thank you, Lord, for freedom to choose,
   and teach me to use it wisely.

Amen.

The stale loaf

It looked all right,
   as good as the day I'd bought it,
   but when I took a bite I realised otherwise,
   the bread dry and hard,
   impossible to eat.

I too grow stale, Lord,
   the freshness that marked my early years of faith
   sometimes seeming a memory,
   a shadow of what it once was and ought to be.
My spirit shrivels up,
   hardened by exposure to the realities of life,
   and I become set in my ways,
   closed to new ideas and experiences —
   closed to you.
Where discipleship is desiccated and commitment withered,
   restore vitality,
   putting a new heart and right spirit within me.

Amen.

The piece of music

It stirred my heart,
   bringing a lump to my throat,
   the emotions it aroused so powerful,
   almost overwhelming,
   that my spirit soared with the melody,
   transported to new heights,
   an ecstasy of delight.

May the same be true, Lord, of knowing you,
   your presence causing me to catch my breath in wonder,
   to exult and marvel.
Instead of being an arid issue of the mind —
   an intellectual assent to truth —
   may faith be an affair of the heart,
   capturing my imagination,
   lifting me up and transporting me into your presence,
   so that, overwhelmed with joy and filled with awe,
   my spirit may rise to you each day,
   in rapturous praise and grateful worship.

Amen.

The stain

I tried everything —
   rinsing, rubbing,
   soaking, scrubbing —
   but to no avail.
It was still there,
   an ugly stain,
   impossible to miss,
   hard to ignore.

The blots in my life, Lord, are equally unsightly,
   too many to number,
   too many to hide.
I strive in vain to remove them,
   to conquer their hold or conceal their presence,
   but try as I might they still show through,
   impossible to hide.
Take what I am, Lord —
   with all the dirt that sticks so closely,
   the ingrained grime that stains my soul —
   and, by your grace, wash me,
   and make me clean.

Amen.

The ornament

It was an attractive piece, there's no denying it —
 not just any old tat,
 but carefully crafted,
 artistic and elegant,
 yet it had no purpose other than to enhance the décor,
 filling an otherwise empty space.
It was for show only,
 intentionally so,
 its function simply to please the eye.

Lord, I know appearances matter,
 but you call me to practical commitment
 rather than ornamental discipleship,
 to a faith that makes a difference.
Save me from showy discipleship
 that's more froth than substance.
Show me what you would have me do
 and help me to do it,
 that I may be not only pleasing in your sight
 but also useful in your service.

Amen.

The refuse collection

They lined the streets,
   regiments of wheelie bins on their weekly parade,
   waiting to be relieved of their load and returned to duty.
Another day's work completed,
   another week's rubbish consigned to the tip.
An unglamorous business, perhaps,
   but as I watched the refuse lorry trundle on its way
   I asked myself where we'd be without it,
   what dirt, disease, stench and squalor would take hold
   had we no such simple service.

Lord, there's all kinds of rubbish in my life too,
   emotional baggage and mental clutter that I should have
   discarded long since,
   but that I've allowed to build up inside,
   suffocating,
   scarring,
   polluting,
   poisoning.
Help me to recognise the litter in my life
   that disfigures and despoils,
   and teach me to dispose of it
   before it disposes of me.

Amen.

The dispensing machine

Tea,
  coffee,
  soup,
  chocolate —
  just a small selection of the drinks on offer.
Insert coins . . .
  select option . . .
  wait.

Lord, I treat **you** like a dispensing machine sometimes,
  as if all I have to do is press the right buttons
  and you will pander to my wishes.
A drop of devotion and touch of faith,
  with a hint of penitence thrown in,
  and you're bound to come up with the goods,
  whatever I may ask.
Forgive me for seeking to exploit rather than worship you,
  and teach me to focus on what I can give
  instead of dwelling on what I might receive.

Amen.